THE BEST 50
APPLE RECIPES

Joanna White

BRISTOL PUBLISHING ENTERPRISES
San Leandro, California

Printed in the United States of America.

ISBN 1-55867-126-9

Cover design: Paredes Design Associates
Cover photography: John A. Benson
Food stylist: Suzanne Carreiro

ALL ABOUT APPLES

Americans have a passion for apples that has resulted in dishes ranging from simple apple butter to sophisticated apple tarte tatin. Now we are lucky to have many varieties available from different regions of the country. Some apples are known for their crisp eating qualities, while others are best cooked into sauces. Still others retain their shape when they are cooked, which makes them ideal for baking. The trick is to select the type of apple best suited to your needs.

NUTRITIONAL INFORMATION

For one medium-sized apple (about 5.5 oz.):

Calories	80	Potassium	170 mg
Carbohydrate	18 g	Protein	0 g
Cholesterol	0 mg	Sodium	0 mg
Dietary Fiber	5 g	Vitamin C	6 mg
Fat	1 g		

STORAGE AND HANDLING

Temperature: Keep apples in a highly humid environment (ideally 90%) and at a temperature close to 32°F without actually being frozen. Home- stored apples should stay good for 4 to 6 months. If the apples lose their crispness, they may still be used for cooking.

Preparation: To minimize oxidation (browning), prepare apples just before serving or protect cut apples by dipping them in a solution of 1 part lemon juice and 3 parts water.

Protection: Keep away from foods with strong odors. Handle as little as possible to avoid skin damage and bruising.

C.A. Storage: Means controlled atmosphere storage, which is a commercial storage method of placing apples in a large airtight refrigerated room where temperature, oxygen, carbon dioxide and humidity are carefully controlled to slow ripening. Apples stay firm and crisp for months.

Freezing: If planning to use apples for cooking after freezing, peel, core and slice apples and immediately store in airtight containers. If planning to use raw after freezing, place peeled, cored and sliced apples in a solution of 1 part lemon juice (or ascorbic acid powder) and 3 parts water, drain and place in an airtight container.

Drying: Wash, peel (if desired), core and slice into $1/4$-inch slices or rounds. Soak in an ascorbic acid (or lemon juice) bath for 2 to 3 minutes, drain and place in a dehydrator. Dry for approximately 6 to 8 hours at 100°F. or until slightly crisp. For apple leathers, puree fruit, add spices (if desired) and spread on a plastic sheet. Dry for approximately 16 to 18 hours at 100°F.

Rehydrating: Cover with hot water and soak for about 15 minutes; drain.

CHOOSING APPLES

- Make sure color is good for the particular variety.
- Choose apples free of brownish spots.
- For red apples, the background color should be slightly yellowish-green (avoid dark green).

- Apples should be firm to the touch; if apples are soft, it usually means that they are mealy and bland.

VARIETIES (listed in alphabetical order)

Cortland: two-toned red and green, snowy white flesh, somewhat flat and oval-shaped; slightly tart, mild flavor. Excellent for eating raw, and good as a baking and sauce apple. Available: Oct. - Jan.

Criterion: sweet, yellow, often with red blush. Good for eating raw, in salads and baking. Flesh stays white longer than other apples. Available: Oct. - Spring.

Gala: yellow to red; good full flavor. Good for eating raw and in salads. Available: Sept. - Dec.

Golden Delicious: mellow, sweet and yellow. Good for eating raw, in salads and baking. Available: year-round.

Granny Smith: green, tart, crisp and juicy. Good for eating raw, in salads and cooking. Available: year-round.

Gravenstein: pale yellow flushed with broad bands of orange-red, tangy-sweet flavor, crisp and juicy. Good for eating raw, cooking and baking. Available: July - Sept.

Jonathan: deep red, mildly tart, crisp and juicy. Excellent for eating raw and cooking, but not good for baking. Available: Sept. - Jan.

McIntosh: whitish yellow flushed with crimson; slightly tart, juicy and aromatic. Good for eating raw and cooking but not good for baking. Available: Sept. - June.

Newton Pippin: light green, crisp and tart. Excellent for eating raw, in salads, cooking and baking. Available: Oct. - June.

Red Delicious: bright to dark red, sometimes striped, mildly sweet and juicy. Good for eating raw. Available: year-round.

Rome Beauty: brilliant red and round. Holds shape well when cooked, good for baking. Available: Oct. - June.

Stayman: purplish-red skin, mildly tart and firm. Excellent for eating raw, also good for baking, cooking and making cider. Available: Oct. - March.

Winesap: dark red, spicy and slightly tart. Good for eating raw, making cider and cooking. Available: Oct. - Aug.

York Imperial: deep red, sometimes with green stripes; has tart, musky flavor and characteristic lopsided shape. Good for baking and cooking, but not eating raw. Available: Oct. - April.

COOKING METHODS
Fruit Syrup (for whole or quartered apples)

For every pound of apples, dissolve $\frac{1}{4}$ cup sugar in 1 cup water. Add a strip of lemon peel for flavor and boil for 2 minutes.

Poaching Fruit

Peel and core the fruit, leave whole or cut in half (or quarters). Immerse in *Fruit Syrup* with rounded part of the fruit at the bottom of the pan. Let the syrup boil up and over the fruit, and then reduce the heat. Cover and let cook over low heat for 15 to 20 minutes or until fruit is transparent. Let fruit cool in syrup.

APPLE SOUP

*This can be used as a starter course or more
commonly as a light dessert.*

6 large apples (prefer Golden Delicious)
1 qt. water
¾ cup sugar
½ tsp. cinnamon
¼ tsp. nutmeg
½ cup lemon juice
1 cup whipping cream
⅔ cup white wine

Peel, core and slice 5 of the 6 apples and place in a saucepan with water. Cook until soft. Puree in a food processor or blender to make applesauce. Add sugar, cinnamon and nutmeg and stir to blend. Peel and core remaining apple, shred and mix with lemon juice. Stir into applesauce and chill. To serve, blend cream and wine into applesauce and serve.

CHEDDAR APPLE SOUP

Makes 8 servings

*The flavor of this creamy fruit soup is sharpened
with the addition of cheese. Calvados is a dry apple brandy.*

¼ cup butter
6 tart apples, peeled, cored and chopped
1 tbs. Calvados or cognac
1 tsp. sugar
4 cups chicken stock
¼ tsp. nutmeg
⅛ tsp. cinnamon
⅛ tsp. white pepper
1 cup cream
2 egg yolks, beaten, or ½ cup cream
¼ tsp. crushed garlic
1 cup fresh breadcrumbs, crusts removed
⅓ cup vegetable oil
3 cups grated sharp cheddar cheese
2 tbs. grated Parmesan cheese

Melt butter in a heavy saucepan, add apples, Calvados and sugar and cook over low heat for 10 minutes. Add chicken stock and cook until apples are very soft. Pour into a food processor or blender and puree until smooth. Add nutmeg, cinnamon, white pepper and cream. Return to pan and heat to warm.

In a food processor or blender, beat egg yolks with garlic. Add breadcrumbs and with machine running, slowly pour oil into egg yolk mixture. Add cheese and process until smooth. Ladle soup into bowls and top with a spoonful of cheese mixture.

FILLED APPLES IN GELATIN

Makes 6 servings

This is an unusual salad, with stuffed apples set in lemon gelatin.

8 cups water
3 tbs. light vinegar or lemon juice
6 large apples
2 tbs. grated fresh lemon peel (zest)
1 cup sugar
1 cup Sauterne
1 pkg. (3 oz.) lemon gelatin
1/2 cup golden raisins
1/3 cup chopped red candied cherries
1/2 cup walnuts or pecans, toasted, optional

Place 6 cups of the water and all of the vinegar (or lemon juice) in a bowl. Peel apples and core, leaving about a 3/4-inch shell. Reserve apple pulp (without cores) and set aside. Place apples in vinegar water while preparing cooking liquid.

Place remaining 2 cups water, lemon peel, sugar and ¾ cup of the Sauterne in a large, shallow saucepan. Heat to a boil and cook until sugar is dissolved, about 5 minutes. Arrange apples in pan and cook over low heat for about 10 to 15 minutes; turn apples over and cook for an additional 10 to 15 minutes or until apples are tender but not mushy. Remove from cooking liquid and chill thoroughly. Reserve cooking liquid.

Prepare lemon gelatin according to package directions, but substitute remaining ¼ cup Sauterne for ¼ cup of the cold water. Chill while preparing filling.

Finely mince reserved apple pulp and add to a small saucepan with raisins, cherries and about ¼ cup of the sugared liquid used for cooking apples. Cook until raisins are plumped. Add nuts (if desired) and fill center of chilled apples. Place apples in a shallow serving dish with sides and pour all but ½ cup gelatin over apples. Beat remaining gelatin with a beater or fork and spoon around edge for a decorative garnish.

 **FRUIT SALAD WITH BRANDY** *Makes 10-12 servings*

Brandy adds a distinctive taste to this wonderful mixture of fruits.
Allowing it to chill overnight helps to develop the flavor.

1/4 cup water
3 tbs. lemon juice
3 large tart apples, peeled, cored and coarsely chopped
3 ripe pears, peeled, cored and coarsely chopped
3 oranges, peeled
1/2 lb. seedless green grapes
1/2 lb. fresh cherries, pitted
1 small honeydew melon, peeled, seeded and chopped
3/4-1 cup confectioners' sugar
1 cup Sauterne wine
1/2 cup brandy

Mix water and lemon juice together in a bowl and add apples and pears. Stir to coat fruit thoroughly. Cut orange segments away from membrane and place in a serving bowl with grapes, cherries and honeydew. Add apple mixture and stir to combine. Sprinkle with confectioners' sugar (amount depends on tartness of fruit; taste and adjust sweetness). Mix Sauterne and brandy together and pour over fruits. Allow to chill overnight before serving. If desired, sprinkle with a little confectioners' sugar before serving.

 **FROZEN FRUIT SALAD** *Makes 8 servings*

*This salad is refreshing, especially when it's hot weather,
or with a heavy meal.*

2 eggs, beaten
½ cup sugar
1 tbs. lemon juice
dash salt
1 can (8 oz.) crushed pineapple, drained, juice reserved
½ cup mayonnaise
½ cup cream
2½ cups diced red apples with peel
⅔ cup diced celery
½ cup chopped walnuts or pecans, toasted
½ cup miniature marshmallows, optional

In a saucepan, mix together eggs, sugar, lemon juice, salt and reserved pineapple juice and simmer over low heat until mixture is slightly thickened. Remove from heat and chill. Stir in mayonnaise. Whip cream until stiff and fold in. Place remaining ingredients in a bowl and gently fold in mayonnaise-cream mixture. Taste and adjust seasonings.

Line a 6-cup mold or loaf pan with plastic wrap and pour in mixture. Freeze for at least 4 hours or overnight. Unmold and serve surrounded with sliced fresh fruit for garnish.

 **CREAMY APPLE AND ENDIVE SALAD**   *Makes 4 servings*

This makes an elegant salad because endive is so dear, so save this one for people who would appreciate it.

4 heads endive
2 apples, (prefer Granny Smith or Golden Delicious)
½ cup chopped walnuts, toasted
¾ cup cream
1 tsp. Dijon mustard
2 tsp. sugar
1 tbs. red wine vinegar (prefer balsamic)
salt and pepper to taste

Clean endive, core and cut into 1-inch pieces. Peel, core and slice apples. Mix endive, apples and walnuts together in a bowl and set aside. With a mixer, whip cream and gently fold in remaining ingredients. Taste and adjust seasonings. Pour dressing over salad mixture, stir and serve.

APPLE CHEESE BREAD

This tasty, moist bread has a subtle flavor.

½ cup butter
⅔ cup sugar
2 eggs, slightly beaten
2 cups flour
1 tsp. baking powder
½ tsp. baking soda

½ tsp. salt
1½ cups grated apples
¾ cup grated cheddar cheese
½ cup chopped walnuts or
  pecans

Beat butter, sugar and eggs together until fluffy. Sift flour, baking powder, baking soda and salt together and mix with apples. Add apple mixture to butter mixture. Stir in cheddar cheese and nuts.

Pour mixture into a greased loaf pan. Bake in a 350° oven for 50 to 60 minutes or until firm in the center. Cool for 5 to 10 minutes in pan. Remove from pan and cool on a wire rack.

APPLE CINNAMON MUFFINS

These are easy to make and very tasty.

1 cup all-purpose flour
½ cup whole wheat flour
½ cup brown sugar, firmly packed
2 tsp. baking powder
½ tsp. cinnamon
¼ tsp. salt
⅓ cup apple juice
¼ cup vegetable oil
1 egg, slightly beaten
1¼ cups finely chopped peeled apples
¼ cup brown sugar, firmly packed
1 tsp. cinnamon

In a bowl, mix together flours, brown sugar, baking powder, cinnamon and salt. In a separate bowl, combine apple juice, oil and egg. Add wet ingredients to flour mixture and stir just to combine (do not overmix). Gently stir in apples. Spoon into greased muffin cups. Mix 1/4 cup brown sugar with 1 tsp. cinnamon and sprinkle over muffin batter. Bake in a 400° oven for 15 minutes or until a wooden pick inserted in the center comes out clean. Cool slightly before removing from muffin tin.

# APPLE BRAN MUFFINS

This is a great recipe for a crowd. Batter can be refrigerated for days.

1 cup raisins or chopped dates
1 cup oatmeal
1 cup boiling water
2 eggs, beaten
1 cup sugar
½ cup vegetable oil
2 cups buttermilk
1 tsp. cinnamon
1 tbs. baking soda
½ tsp. salt
1½ cups flour
1½ cups whole wheat flour
2 cups all-bran cereal
1 cup finely diced peeled apples
1 cup walnuts or pecans
warmed honey glaze, optional

In a bowl, mix raisins (or dates), oatmeal and boiling water together and let stand. In a separate bowl, combine eggs, sugar, oil and buttermilk and stir into raisin mixture. Mix together cinnamon, baking soda, salt, flour and all-bran cereal. Stir into batter with apples and walnuts, just barely mixing. Fill greased muffin cups ¾ full. Bake in a 375° oven for 20 minutes. If desired, glaze tops of muffins with warmed honey just as they come out of the oven.

EBLESKIVER (DANISH APPLE CAKES)

Makes 24

*Ebleskiver (or aebleskiver) is a national specialty dish of Denmark.
You need an ebleskiver pan to do these properly. Apple slices are
baked in a light waffle-type dough in the form of a sphere and
dusted with powdered sugar. Alternative fillings can be used such as
applesauce, apple butter, jams, or even peanut butter.*

2 eggs, separated
1 tbs. sugar
¼ tsp. salt
1 cup flour
½ tsp. baking soda
½ tsp. baking powder
dash ground cardamom
1 cup buttermilk
¼ cup butter
3-4 cups peeled apple slices or chopped apples
confectioners' sugar for dusting

With a mixer, beat egg yolks until light yellow in color. Add sugar and salt and mix. Sift flour, baking soda, baking powder and cardamom together; add to egg mixture alternately with buttermilk. Beat egg whites until stiff. Gently fold into batter.

Heat an ebleskiver pan. Place ½ tsp. butter in each cup and heat until foamy. Drop batter into cups, filling each about ⅔ full. Place apple slices or chopped apples in center of each cup. Cook over medium heat until browned and crisp on the bottom. Turn each cake with a fork (or knitting needle) to cook other side. Remove cakes from pan and sprinkle with confectioners' sugar. Serve warm.

APPLE MOCHA BREAD

Makes 1 loaf

*This makes a moist bread and offers a surprising taste experience.
Great served with tea or latte.*

½ cup strong coffee, chilled
1 tsp. baking soda
1½ cups flour
½ tsp. salt
½ tsp. ground cloves
1 tsp. cinnamon
½ cup butter

1 cup sugar
2 eggs
1 oz. unsweetened chocolate,
 melted
1 cup grated peeled apples
½ cup raisins

Line a loaf pan with brown paper or parchment paper. Grease paper and sides of loaf pan. Mix coffee and baking soda together. In a bowl, combine flour, salt, cloves and cinnamon. With a mixer, beat butter and sugar together until fluffy. Beat in eggs. Stir in chocolate. Add flour mixture alternately with coffee mixture to butter mixture. Stir in apples and raisins. Pour batter into prepared pan and bake in a 350° oven for 50 to 60 minutes. Cool for 10 minutes before turning out.

Makes 1 loaf

APPLE WHOLE WHEAT NUT BREAD

*Here's a wholesome treat to serve as an after-school snack
with cider or milk, or have a slice with tea.*

1/4 cup butter
1/2 cup sugar
1 egg
1 cup grated peeled apples
1/4 cup apple juice
1 1/2 cups whole wheat flour
1 1/2 cups all-purpose flour

1/2 tsp. salt
1 tsp. baking soda
1 cup buttermilk
1 tbs. grated fresh orange peel
 (zest)
1 cup chopped walnuts or pecans

Cover the bottom of a loaf pan with brown paper and grease paper and sides well. With a mixer, cream butter and sugar together. Add egg and beat well. Beat in apples and apple juice. Sift together flours, salt and baking soda. Beat into butter mixture alternately with buttermilk. Beat in orange zest and nuts. Pour into prepared pan and bake in a 350° oven for 1 to 1 1/4 hours or until a knife inserted in the center comes out clean. Let cool in pan.

PUMPKIN-APPLE BREAD

Makes 1 loaf

Apple adds moisture to this spicy pumpkin bread.

¼ cup butter
1 cup sugar
2 eggs
1 cup canned pumpkin
½ cup milk
2 cups flour
2 tsp. baking powder
½ tsp. baking soda

1 tsp. salt
1 tsp. cinnamon
½ tsp. nutmeg
pinch ground cloves
1¼ cups grated peeled apples
1 cup chopped walnuts or
   pecans, optional

Line a loaf pan with brown paper. Grease paper and sides of pan well. With a mixer, cream butter and sugar together. Add eggs, pumpkin and milk and beat well. Sift together flour, baking powder, baking soda, salt, cinnamon, nutmeg and cloves. Add dry ingredients to pumpkin mixture, mixing well. Stir in apples, and nuts if desired. Pour into prepared pan and bake in a 350° oven for 50 to 60 minutes or until a knife inserted in the center comes out clean.

DUTCH BABY WITH APPLES

A Dutch baby is a rich, "eggy" pancake that is poured into a hot pan and baked so it puffs. An alternative to apple filling is a sprinkling of confectioners' sugar and a squeeze of fresh lemon juice.

⅓ cup butter
4 eggs
1 cup milk
1 cup flour
1 tbs. grated fresh lemon peel (zest)

2 apples, peeled, cored and sliced
1 tsp. lemon juice
2 tbs. butter
sugar to taste
dash cinnamon

Place ⅓ cup butter in a 3-quart baking dish or oven-safe skillet and set in oven to heat. In a food processor or blender, whirl eggs for 1 minute, pour in milk and mix. Add flour and lemon peel. Blend for 30 seconds and immediately pour into hot buttered pan. Bake in a 425° oven until well browned, about 20 to 25 minutes.

To prepare filling, mix apple slices with lemon juice. Heat butter in a skillet and sauté apple slices with sugar until soft, but still hold shape. Season with cinnamon and serve on top of Dutch pancake.

APPLE PANCAKES

Apples add interest, flavor and moisture to common pancakes. Different flours, such as barley flour or millet flour, can be used to create unique flavors and make a delightful change from wheat.

1½ cups all-purpose flour
½ tsp. salt
1 tbs. baking powder
1¼ cups buttermilk or milk
2 eggs, beaten

1 tbs. vegetable oil
2 cups chopped peeled apples
2 tbs. sugar, optional
½ tsp. cinnamon, optional

Mix flour, salt, baking powder, buttermilk, eggs and oil together in bowl and stir with a fork until just barely mixed. If you prefer a thinner batter, add a little more buttermilk. In a separate bowl, mix apples with sugar and cinnamon. Heat a nonstick skillet over medium high heat, spray with nonstick vegetable spray (if needed), spread pancake batter into rounds and sprinkle with apple mixture. Press apples slightly into batter. Cook until golden on bottom and turn, cook other side to golden brown and serve immediately.

Makes 8 servings **PORK TENDERLOIN WITH APPLES**

This incredibly delicious entrée is quick and easy to fix.
It goes well with a rice accompaniment.

4 lb. pork tenderloins
½ cup butter
1 large onion, chopped
2 Golden Delicious apples,
  peeled and chopped

¾ cup mango chutney
2 cups cream
2 tsp. Dijon mustard
½-¾ tsp. curry powder
salt and pepper to taste

Cut tenderloins into ½-inch slices. In a large skillet, melt butter and quickly sauté pork medallions for 1-2 minutes. Remove medallions and set aside. Sauté onion in skillet until golden, add apples and cook until tender.

Stir in chutney and cream. Cook for several minutes to thicken sauce. Add mustard, curry, salt and pepper. Return meat to pan and heat through. Serve immediately.

APPLES AND CHICKEN IN PHYLLO

Makes 12 servings

Working with phyllo dough can be a little tricky, but the result is an elegant entrée. A light lemon dessert would be an excellent finale.

6 chicken breast halves, boned and skinned
salt and pepper to taste
3 tart apples, peeled, cored and sliced
1 tbs. lemon juice
2 tbs. butter
12 oz. Appenzeller or Swiss cheese, cut into strips
½ lb. unsalted butter
12 phyllo sheets
12 tsp. cold butter

Cut chicken into strips and season with salt and pepper. Mix apples with lemon juice. In a skillet, melt 2 tbs. butter and sauté apple slices until almost soft. Remove apples and set aside. In same skillet, sauté chicken strips until chicken is firm to the touch but not thoroughly cooked.

Clarify unsalted butter by melting over medium heat. Skim foam from top and let milky residue settle on bottom of pan. Carefully pour off clear liquid.

Place phyllo sheets on counter and cover with a slightly damp tea towel. (This will help keep the pastry from drying out while working with it). Remove one sheet of phyllo at a time. Brush half the sheet with clarified butter and fold in half widthwise. Turn sheet so that narrow end faces you and brush with butter. Put 1 tsp. cold butter about 2 inches from end. Top with chicken strips, apples slices and cheese slices. Roll over once and fold in sides. Brush with melted butter. Roll all the way up and brush top and sides with butter. Place on a parchment-lined baking sheet with sides. Repeat, keeping rolls in refrigerator until ready to bake.

Place chilled phyllo rolls in a 400° oven and bake for 25 to 30 minutes or until golden brown. Serve immediately.

APPLES WITH PORK CHOPS

Makes 6 servings

Apples are a perfect complement to pork. In this recipe, the apples (Pippin work best) are glazed under a broiler.

3 large, tart apples, peeled
1 tbs. lemon juice
3 tbs. white or brown sugar
1/4 cup butter, melted
1 1/2 cups dry white wine
3/4 cup apple brandy
1 tsp. cinnamon
6 pork chops, 1-inch thick
salt and pepper to taste
4 tbs. butter
2 tbs. vegetable oil
2 tbs. flour
2 beef bouillon cubes
1/4 cup hot water
chopped parsley for garnish

Core and slice apples; combine in a bowl with lemon juice and 1 tbs. of the sugar. Transfer to a buttered shallow baking dish. Sprinkle with melted butter, 1/2 cup wine and 1/4 cup brandy. Mix remaining 2 tbs. sugar and cinnamon together and sprinkle on top of apples. Place under a broiler, about 8 inches from element, and cook for about 20 minutes or until apples are golden. Watch carefully.

Sprinkle pork chops with salt and pepper. Heat 2 tbs. of the butter and 1 tbs. of the oil in a skillet. Quickly brown chops on both sides. Add 1/2 cup wine and 1/4 cup brandy. Bring to a boil, reduce heat, cover and cook for 20 minutes. Remove chops and keep warm.

In same skillet, add remaining 2 tbs. butter and 1 tbs. oil and stir to loosen particles in bottom of pan. Add flour and stir to make a paste (roux). Add remaining wine and brandy and stir until smooth. Mix bouillon cubes with hot water and add to wine mixture. Cook for 5 minutes, taste and season with salt and pepper. Place chops on a platter, cover with apples, pour sauce on top and sprinkle with parsley.

SWEET POTATO-APPLE CASSEROLE

Makes 6 servings

*This quick-to-fix recipe would go well with a crunchy
tossed salad and a green vegetable like asparagus.*

4 cups sliced sweet potatoes
4 cups sliced, peeled tart apples
¼ cup chopped onion
2 tsp. salt
½ cup maple syrup
1 cup apple juice
½ cup butter, melted
1½ lb. breakfast sausage meat

Grease a 2-quart casserole. Alternately layer sweet potatoes and apple slices, sprinkling a little onion and salt between layers. Combine maple syrup, apple juice and butter and pour over layered apples and potatoes. Cover and bake in a 350° oven for 1 hour. In a skillet, brown sausage and drain off excess fat. Sprinkle crumbled sausage over casserole and bake, uncovered, for an additional 10 minutes. Serve hot.

Makes 4 servings

VERMONT APPLES AND SAUSAGE

This dish can be served as a breakfast entrée, or serve it for dinner with brown bread, baked beans and tossed salad.

1 lb. pork sausage (links or patties)
1 cup pure maple syrup
½ cup cider vinegar
4 large apples, cored and cut into ½-inch rings

Fry sausage until golden brown, drain and keep warm in a 200° oven while preparing apples. In a skillet, mix syrup and vinegar together, heat to warm and add apple rings. Simmer uncovered until apples are tender-crisp, about 5 minutes. Arrange apple rings on a platter with sausage, pour syrup mixture over all and serve immediately.

APPLE PRUNE STUFFING

Makes 4 cups

This stuffing is ideal for goose, chicken, turkey or even pork roasts. There is enough here for an 8 lb. bird.

1 cup pitted prunes
boiling water to cover
1 cup chopped apples
4 slices bread, crusts removed
1 cup chopped pecans, toasted
1 egg, beaten
1/4 cup butter, melted
salt and pepper to taste

Cover prunes with boiling water and soak for 15 minutes. Drain off water and chop prunes; place in a bowl. Cut bread into small cubes and add to prunes. Gently stir in remaining ingredients. Taste and adjust seasonings.

RED CABBAGE AND APPLES

This popular vegetable dish goes well with heavy meat meals.

2 tbs. butter
1 medium-sized red cabbage, finely shredded
1/4 cup honey or firmly packed brown sugar
1 small onion, finely chopped
2 apples, peeled, cored and finely chopped
1/4 cup red wine
3-4 tbs. lemon juice
salt and pepper to taste, optional

Melt butter in a skillet and sauté cabbage and honey or brown sugar for several minutes. Add onion, apples, wine and lemon juice and bring to a boil. Reduce heat, cover and simmer for 45 minutes to 1 hour. Taste and add salt and pepper if desired. Adjust seasonings and serve.

BAKED APPLES WITH SAUSAGE

Makes 6 servings

*Serve this as a breakfast dish with eggs or
as a great side dish for a roast dinner.*

6 large tart apples, unpeeled
1 cup cooked highly seasoned sausage meat
1/4 cup brown sugar

Cut top off apples and remove center, leaving a 3/4-inch shell. Chop up apple pulp (without core) and add sausage meat. Stuff sausage inside apple hollow and place on a baking dish. Sprinkle apples with brown sugar. Bake in a 375° oven until tender, about 30 minutes.

CARROT AND APPLE BAKE

This is a good substitute for candied yams. It's great served with baked ham or pork roast. Golden Delicious apples work particularly well in this recipe.

10 carrots, peeled
5 large apples, peeled and cored
1 tsp. lemon juice
3 tbs. butter
6 tbs. brown sugar, firmly packed
salt and pepper to taste

Cut carrots into thin matchstick strips and place in a steamer basket. Cut apples into thick slices, toss in lemon juice and add to steamer basket. Steam carrots and apples until just slightly tender. Remove from basket and transfer to a buttered 9-x-13-inch baking pan. Heat butter and brown sugar together in a small saucepan until sugar dissolves; pour over carrot mixture. Sprinkle with salt and pepper. Place in a 350° oven and bake for 25 to 30 minutes or until tender.

PHYLLO APPLE PIE

Flaky phyllo dough is used as the crust for this special apple pie.

1½ cups sugar
¼ cup flour
1½ tsp. cinnamon
¼ tsp. nutmeg
pinch salt
10 cups sliced peeled apples

2 tbs. lemon juice
2 tbs. butter
1½ cups chopped walnuts
12 sheets phyllo
½ cup melted butter

In a bowl, mix sugar, flour, cinnamon, nutmeg and salt together. Sprinkle apples with lemon juice and add to sugar mixture. Add walnuts and stir. Brush a sheet of phyllo with butter and place it in the bottom of a 10-inch pie pan. Repeat with 7 more sheets of phyllo. Place apple mixture in phyllo lining and dot with butter. Brush each remaining phyllo sheet with butter and arrange on top of apples. With scissors, trim edge all around pie, leaving a 2-inch overhang. Fold overhang under, forming a small ridge. Cut a small hole in the center of pie to allow steam to escape. Bake in a 375° oven for 50 to 60 minutes or until crust is golden.

APPLE-BLUEBERRY COBBLER

Cobbler is a treat for breakfast or dessert. Serve it hot or warm with a dollop of whipped cream or ice cream.

1 cup flour
¾ cup sugar
1 tsp. baking powder
¾ tsp. salt
½ tsp. ground mace or nutmeg
1 egg, beaten
2 cups fresh or frozen blueberries

3 apples, peeled and sliced
  (prefer Granny Smith)
2 tbs. brown sugar
⅓ cup butter, melted
3 tbs. sugar
½ tsp. cinnamon

Butter a 9-x-13-inch baking dish. In a bowl, combine flour, sugar, baking powder, salt and mace (or nutmeg). Stir in beaten egg. In a separate bowl, toss blueberries, apples slices and brown sugar together. Sprinkle the bottom of prepared baking dish with fruit mixture and pour batter on top. Pour melted butter over all. Mix sugar and cinnamon together and sprinkle on top. Bake in a 375° oven for 30 minutes or until a knife inserted in the center comes out clean.

# APPLE COCONUT COFFEE CAKE

Makes 12 servings

*A moist, tender cake topped with a sprinkling of almonds
and sugar is delicious served warm for breakfast or brunch.*

¾ cup butter
1 cup sugar
3 eggs
1½ cups flour
2 tsp. baking powder
¼ tsp. salt

½ cup milk
1¼ cups shredded coconut
2 large apples, peeled and diced
  (prefer tart variety)
½ cup sliced almonds
3 tbs. sugar

Grease a 9-x-13-inch baking dish. Using a mixer, cream butter and sugar until smooth. Add eggs and continue to beat well. Mix flour, baking powder and salt together, add to creamed mixture alternately with milk and beat until smooth. Stir in coconut and diced apples. Pour into prepared baking dish and sprinkle top with almonds and 3 tbs. sugar. Bake in a 350° oven for 30 to 35 minutes or until cake springs back when lightly touched.

SPICE APPLE CAKE

This rich-tasting, moist cake is loaded with raisins and walnuts.

½ cup butter
1 cup brown sugar, firmly packed
1 egg
1¾ cups flour
½ tsp. salt
1 tsp. baking soda

¾ tsp. cinnamon
½ tsp. cloves
½ tsp. nutmeg
2 cups coarsely chopped raisins
1 cup chopped walnuts or pecans
1 cup diced peeled apples

Butter a Bundt pan and set aside. With a mixer, cream butter and brown sugar together and add egg; mix well. In a separate bowl, mix flour, salt, baking soda, cinnamon, cloves and nutmeg together. Add ½ cup of flour mixture to raisins and nuts, and stir to coat. Beat remaining dry ingredients into creamed mixture. Add apples and beat. Stir in raisins and nuts and pour into prepared pan. Bake in a 350° oven for 35 to 40 minutes or until a knife inserted in cake comes out clean. Remove from oven, cool for 10 minutes and remove cake from pan.

APPLE TARTE TATIN

Makes 8 servings

This recipe is fairly complicated but produces an elegant dessert, somewhat reminiscent of an upside down apple pie.

CRUST

1 cup flour
1/3 cup cold butter, cut into
  1/4-inch cubes

1 tsp. sugar
1/8 tsp. salt
3 tbs. cold water

FILLING

1/3 cup sugar
1/4 cup water
1/4 cup butter
6 cups sliced apples (prefer
  Golden Delicious or Pippin)

1/3 cup sugar
1 egg, beaten
1/2 cup apricot jam
2 tbs. water, Calvados or cognac
toasted almond slices for garnish

Place flour, butter, sugar, and salt in a large bowl. Mix ingredients together with a pastry cutter until butter pieces are about the size of peas. Add water and gently form into a ball. Roll to about 1/8- or 1/4-inch thick. Set aside.

Mix sugar and water in a saucepan and bring to a boil. Keep boiling until it turns a caramel color, and pour it immediately into a 9-inch pie pan; tilt to coat bottom. Butter sides of pan and set aside.

Melt 1/4 cup butter in a large skillet and add apples and sugar. Sauté for 5 minutes, stirring carefully to avoid breaking apple slices. Pour apple slices onto a cookie sheet. When apples are cool enough to handle, arrange slices over caramel in concentric circles (beginning in the middle), overlapping slices. Continue to arrange in layers until the whole bottom and part of the sides are covered. Fill with remaining apples. Place dough on top and trim so that it comes to edge of apples. Brush with beaten egg and prick dough with a fork. Place pan on a cookie sheet and bake in a 400° oven for 45 minutes or until dough is nicely browned. If dough browns too quickly, cover with foil.

Remove from oven; run a knife around pan rim to loosen crust. Let tarte cool for 5 minutes, place platter on top of pie plate and invert. Tarte should unmold easily. Heat jam and water (or liqueur) until warm, strain through a sieve and brush over apples to glaze. Sprinkle with almond slices.

POACHED APPLES WITH CREME ANGLAISE

This incredible poached apple dessert is covered with cream sauce, drizzled with caramel sauce and topped with macadamia nuts.

6 Golden Delicious apples,
  peeled

¼ cup dried currants
2 cups apple juice

Cut apples into ¼-inch slices. Place apples in a saucepan with currants and apple juice. Bring to a boil, turn heat to low and simmer, covered, until apples are tender but still hold their shape, about 7 minutes. Drain apples and cool.

CREAM SAUCE (CREME ANGLAISE)

1¾ cups milk
6 egg yolks
½ cup sugar

¼ cup cream
1 tsp. vanilla extract

Scald milk and set aside. Place egg yolks and sugar in a bowl and beat until mixture is pale yellow and forms a ribbon. Add hot milk and pour into a saucepan. Place over medium-low heat, stirring with a wooden spoon until mixture coats spoon. Remove from heat; add cream and vanilla. Strain through a sieve and cool.

CARAMEL SAUCE

½ cup butter	½ cup brown sugar
½ cup sugar	½ cup evaporated milk

Melt butter in a saucepan and add sugar, brown sugar and evaporated milk. Stir over medium heat until caramel sauce thickens. Remove from heat until ready to use.

½ cup chopped macadamia nuts, toasted

To assemble: Spoon apple mixture into small bowls, top with cream sauce (creme anglaise), drizzle with caramel sauce and sprinkle with macadamia nuts.

ORIENTAL SPUN APPLES

Makes 6-8 servings

In this unique dessert, apple wedges are battered, deep-fried, dipped in sugar syrup and dropped in ice water to create a hard caramelized coating. The traditional decoration is black sesame seeds, but white sesame seeds can be substituted.

6 apples, peeled and cored
enough water to cover apples
1 tsp. salt
1/4 cup cornstarch
3 eggs, slightly beaten
1/4 flour
oil for deep frying
1/2 cup water
2 cups sugar
2 tbs. sesame oil
1 tbs. black sesame seeds
4 cups ice water

Cut apples into 8 pieces each, place in a bowl with enough water to cover and add salt. In a separate bowl, mix cornstarch with eggs until smooth. Dredge apples in flour and dip in egg batter. Heat oil to 375° and fry apples until golden brown. Remove from oil and keep warm.

Place ½ cup water and sugar in a saucepan and heat to 300° without stirring. Add sesame oil and sesame seeds. Remove from heat. Dip fried apples in sugar syrup and coat well. Immediately drop into ice water until glaze hardens; transfer to an oiled plate. Serve immediately.

# FLAMING APPLE CREPES

Makes 8 servings

The crepe pancakes can be made the day before with waxed paper placed between crepes to keep them from sticking together. The apple filling is best made the day of serving.

4 eggs
1 cup milk
1 cup water
½ tsp. salt
¼ cup butter, melted
2 cups flour

In a food processor or blender, beat eggs well. Beat in milk, water, salt and butter. Beat in flour and allow mixture to rest for 30 minutes. Heat a 6-inch crepe pan over medium heat and brush with oil. Pour about ⅛ cup batter into pan, swirling to cover bottom of pan; pour off any excess. Cook for 30 seconds and turn. Cook briefly and remove from pan. Repeat until all batter is used.

½ cup sugar
2 tbs. flour
¾ tsp. cinnamon
¼ tsp. nutmeg
dash ground cloves
2 tbs. butter
4 apples, peeled and thinly sliced

1 tbs. grated fresh lemon peel
 (zest)
¼ cup brandy
½ cup cream
2 tbs. sugar
½ cup chopped pecans, toasted

In a bowl, combine sugar, flour, cinnamon, nutmeg and cloves. In a saucepan, melt butter, add apples and lemon zest and cook until soft (add water if needed to keep from scorching). Add sugar mixture and stir until thick. Place about 3 to 4 tbs. hot apple mixture down center of each crepe and fold. Place folded crepes side by side in a greased, shallow baking pan. Heat in oven at 375° for 10 minutes.

Heat brandy in a small saucepan and ignite. Immediately pour over crepes and let flame die out. Whip cream, blend in sugar and top each apple crepe with a dollop of sweetened whipped cream. Sprinkle with pecans.

# APPLE STRUDEL

Makes 8 servings

Strudel is made much easier with prepackaged phyllo dough.

CRUMBS

½ cup unseasoned breadcrumbs
½ cup chopped walnuts
½ cup sugar

¼ tsp. nutmeg
¼ tsp. cinnamon

In a small bowl, combine ingredients and mix well; set aside.

APPLE FILLING

2 lb. apples, peeled, cored and
  thinly sliced
½ cup sugar
¼ cup brown sugar, firmly packed
2 tbs. flour
¼ tsp. nutmeg

½ tsp. cinnamon
1 tbs. grated fresh lemon peel
  (zest)
½ cup raisins, plumped in hot
  water and drained

Mix filling ingredients together.

1 pkg. (1 lb.) phyllo dough
3/4 cup butter, melted
2 tbs. butter, firm

Line a jelly roll pan with parchment paper or brown paper. Layer 2 sheets of phyllo at a time in pan, brushing melted butter between layers and on top. Sprinkle with 2 tbs. crumbs. Continue layering with phyllo, brushing with butter and sprinkling with crumbs 5 more times, using 12 sheets in all. Sprinkle remaining crumbs over 1/4 of pastry on short side. Spoon apple filling over crumbs and dot with firm butter. Roll up like a jelly roll as tightly as possible, tucking in ends. Brush with butter and bake in a 375° oven for 1 hour. Cool slightly and serve with *Sour Cream Sauce.*

SOUR CREAM SAUCE

Makes 1 pint

1 pt. sour cream (can use nonfat)   1 tsp. cinnamon
6 tbs. confectioners' sugar, sifted   1/2 tsp. nutmeg

In a bowl, mix all ingredients together until smooth. Refrigerate until ready to use.

APPLE KUCHEN

Makes 8 servings

This is a special breakfast or brunch cake made with yeast and topped with apple slices.

1 tbs. yeast
¾ cup warm water
⅓ cup sugar
2¾ cups flour
2 tbs. nonfat dried milk
3 tbs. butter
1 tsp. salt
2 eggs
½ cup cream
½ cup sugar
2 large apples, peeled, cored and thinly sliced
½ cup sugar mixed with 1 tsp. cinnamon

In a bowl, dissolve yeast in warm water. Add 1/3 cup sugar and about 1/2 cup of the flour and stir to make a sponge. Cover with plastic wrap and place bowl on a warm oven door for 30 minutes. Place remaining flour, nonfat dried milk, butter and salt in a food processor and process for about 10 seconds. Add yeast mixture and 1 egg and process for about 40 seconds. If dough gets too sticky, turn the machine off and let it rest for about 2 minutes before finishing.

Roll dough out into a circle to fit a 8- or 9-inch pan, pressing dough up the sides. Sprinkle with 1/4 cup of the sugar and place apples over dough. Beat cream with the remaining 1/4 cup sugar and 1 egg. Pour over apples. Sprinkle top with cinnamon sugar. Bake in a 350° oven for about 30 minutes or until a knife inserted comes out clean. Cool on a rack.

RAW APPLE CAKE

Makes 12 servings

This very moist cake is loaded with apples and raisins.

2 cups sugar
½ cup vegetable oil
1 tsp. vanilla extract
2 eggs, beaten
2 cups flour
2 tsp. cinnamon

2 tsp. baking soda
1 tsp. salt
1 cup chopped walnuts or pecans
1 cup raisins, plumped in hot
  water and drained
4 cups sliced apples

Grease a 9-x-13-inch pan and set aside. With a mixer, beat sugar, oil and vanilla together until well blended. Add eggs, beating well. In a separate bowl, mix flour, cinnamon, baking soda and salt. Add to sugar mixture and beat until smooth. Stir in nuts and drained raisins. Pour into prepared pan. Place apples in batter in horizontally in rows. Bake in a 350° oven for 50 to 60 minutes or until a knife inserted in the center comes out clean.

APPLE CHARLOTTE

This simple, light dessert is flavored with a touch of brandy.

3 eggs, separated
2/3 cup sugar
pinch salt
2 cups grated peeled apples
1/3 cup matzo meal

1 tbs. grated fresh lemon peel
 (zest)
1 tbs. plum brandy
1/4 tsp. cream of tartar
1/4 cup finely chopped pecans

Grease an 8-inch springform pan. With a mixer, beat egg yolks, sugar and salt until thick and lemon colored. Add apples, matzo meal, lemon peel and brandy and just barely mix in. In a separate bowl, beat egg whites with cream of tartar until stiff. Gently fold beaten whites into yolk mixture and pour into prepared springform pan. Sprinkle with pecans and bake in a 350° oven for 35 minutes or until brown and firm. Cool before removing sides of pan.

# APPLE NUT BAKE

Serve this simple dessert warm with lots of whipped cream on top.

2 eggs
1 cup sugar
1/4 cup flour
2 1/2 tsp. baking powder
1/2 tsp. salt
2 tsp. vanilla extract
1 cup chopped peeled apples
1 cup chopped walnuts or pecans

Grease a 9-inch pie pan. With a mixer, beat eggs well. Add sugar and beat until mixture is a lemon yellow color. Mix flour, baking powder and salt together and beat into egg mixture. Add vanilla, apples and walnuts, stirring to combine. Pour into pie pan and bake in a 350° oven for 35 minutes. Serve warm.

FRENCH APPLE PIE

An apple and raisin filling is covered with brown sugar crumble.
Top with ice cream or frozen yogurt.

7 cups sliced peeled apples	pinch salt
1 tbs. lemon juice	1 premade 9-inch pie crust
1½ tbs. diced maraschino cherries	1 cup flour
2 tbs. raisins	½ cup butter
¾ cup brown sugar, firmly packed	½ cup brown sugar

In a bowl, mix apples with lemon juice and cherries. Plump raisins in hot water and drain. Add plumped raisins to apples with ¾ cup brown sugar and salt. Pour mixture into pie crust. In a separate bowl, combine flour, butter and brown sugar, mixing with a pastry blender to fine crumbs. Sprinkle on top of apples. Bake in a 400° oven for 50 minutes or until golden brown in color.

APPLE CRISP

Makes 6 servings

This dessert is fast and easy to make. Vary with different apples.

5 cups sliced or chopped peeled apples
2 tsp. lemon juice
1/4 cup butter
1 cup brown sugar, firmly packed
1/2 cup flour
1/2 tsp. cinnamon
1/2 tsp. nutmeg
1/4 tsp. salt

Grease a 9-inch pie pan. Mix apples with lemon juice and arrange in bottom of pie pan. Using a pastry blender, mix butter, brown sugar, flour, cinnamon, nutmeg and salt together in a bowl until crumbly. Sprinkle over apples and bake in a 350° oven for 50 minutes or until top is golden brown and apples are tender.

GINGERBREAD APPLE COBBLER

The apples are partially baked, covered with gingerbread batter and baked again. Other fruits can be used in the place of apples, such as peaches or pears. Serve with whipped cream.

4 large apples, peeled, cored and sliced	1 cup flour
1 tbs. lemon juice	½ tsp. salt
½ cup sugar	1 tsp. baking soda
1 egg	½ tsp. baking powder
½ cup buttermilk	½ tsp. ginger
¼ cup molasses	½ tsp. nutmeg
¼ cup sugar	¼ tsp. cinnamon
	1½ tbs. butter, melted

Grease an 8-inch square pan. Mix apples with lemon juice and sugar, and place in pan. Bake in a 350° oven for 20 minutes.

With a mixer, beat egg. Add buttermilk, molasses and sugar; beat. Sift flour, salt, soda, baking powder, ginger, nutmeg and cinnamon together. Beat dry ingredients and butter into egg mixture. Pour batter over apples and bake for an additional 30 minutes. Serve warm.

BEST APPLE PIE

*The variety of apples can make all the difference in the world
in the flavor and juiciness of apple pie.*

CRUST
(makes 1 double crust)

2 cups flour
1/4 tsp. salt
3/4 cup butter
3 tbs. shortening
1/2 cup cold water

Place flour, salt, butter and shortening in a bowl and mix together with a pastry blender until butter is the size of small peas. Add water and stir with a fork to mix. Quickly press together into a ball, cover and refrigerate for at least 1/2 hour before rolling. Roll 1/2 of the dough out and line a 9-inch pie pan. Roll remaining dough for top crust and set aside.

FILLING

9 tart apples (prefer Pippin or Granny Smiths)
2 tbs. lemon juice
1 tbs. grated fresh lemon peel (zest)
$\frac{1}{2}$-$\frac{3}{4}$ cup sugar
1 tbs. flour
1 tsp. cinnamon
dash nutmeg, optional
3 tbs. butter

Peel, core and thinly slice apples. Place in a bowl with lemon juice and lemon zest. Mix together sugar, flour, cinnamon and nutmeg (if desired); add to apples and stir. Place apples in pastry-lined pie pan. Cut butter into small pieces and sprinkle over apples. Cover with top crust, slicing small vent holes, and seal and crimp rim. Bake in a 350° oven for 45 minutes or until crust is golden brown.

 **CRANBERRY APPLE CRISP** *Makes 8 servings*

When cranberries are in season, take advantage of their healthy nutrients. Apples help to sweeten the tartness of cranberries.

3 lb. apples, peeled, cored and diced
12 oz. fresh cranberries
½ cup sugar
2 tsp. cinnamon
1 tsp. allspice
1½ tbs. orange liqueur
1 tbs. cornstarch
1 tsp. quick-cooking tapioca
1 cup oats
½ cup brown sugar, firmly packed
⅓ cup chopped walnuts, peanuts or pecans
¼ cup butter
1 tsp. cinnamon
¼ tsp. nutmeg

Butter an 8-inch square pan. Place apples, cranberries, sugar, cinnamon and allspice in a saucepan and cook over medium heat for 5 minutes, stirring constantly. Mix liqueur with cornstarch and tapioca and stir into cooking fruit. Reduce heat and simmer for 2 minutes. Pour mixture into prepared pan.

In a bowl, combine remaining ingredients and mix until crumbly. Sprinkle over fruit. Bake in a 350° oven for about 20 minutes or until topping is golden brown. Serve with ice cream or sweetened whipped cream.

APPLE BARS

*You could serve this old-fashioned type of cookie for dessert
by cutting slightly larger squares and serving hot with a
dollop of whipped cream or ice cream.*

4 cups thinly sliced peeled apples
¼ cup water
sugar to taste, optional (depending on tartness of apples)
cinnamon and nutmeg to taste
¾ cup butter
1 cup brown sugar, firmly packed
1¾ cups flour
½ tsp. baking soda
1 tsp. salt
1½ cups rolled oats

Place apples, water and sugar in a saucepan and cook over low heat until apples are quite soft. If needed, add more water to keep apples from scorching. Remove apples and place in food processor or blender to make into applesauce consistency. Add cinnamon and nutmeg to taste.

Grease and flour a 9-x-13-inch pan. With a mixer, beat butter and brown sugar together. Sift flour with soda and salt and add to butter mixture; beat until well incorporated. Stir in rolled oats. Press ½ of the crumb mixture in bottom of prepared pan. Spread with applesauce mixture. Cover with remaining crumb mixture, patting lightly. Bake for 25 to 30 minutes in a 375° oven or until lightly browned. Cool slightly before cutting.

 **APPLE PUDDING**

Old-fashioned creamy pudding is baked on crushed graham crackers.

8 tart apples, cored and sliced	1 pt. sour cream
1 cup sugar	1 tsp. vanilla extract
1/4 cup butter	dash nutmeg
6 eggs, beaten	2 cups graham cracker crumbs

In a saucepan, combine apples, 1/2 cup of the sugar and all of the butter; cook over low heat until apples are soft. In a double boiler or heavy saucepan, cook egg, sour cream and remaining 1/2 cup sugar, stirring constantly until thickened. Remove from heat and stir in vanilla and nutmeg. Gently stir in apples.

Butter an 8-inch pan. Reserve 1/3 cup graham cracker crumbs, and sprinkle remaining crumbs in bottom of pan; press down with hands. Cover with apple mixture and sprinkle with remaining crumbs. Place in a 325° oven and bake for 1 hour.

APPLE CRANBERRY RELISH

This colorful relish is ideal for the holiday season.

8 cups diced peeled apples
12 oz. fresh cranberries
1 cup water
2 cups sugar
$\frac{1}{4}$ cup cornstarch

In a heavy-bottomed saucepan over medium heat, cook apples, cranberries, water and 1 cup sugar of the sugar together for 5 minutes, stirring occasionally. Mix remaining 1 cup sugar with cornstarch and add to saucepan, stirring until sugar is dissolved and juice is clear. Cool and refrigerate until ready to serve.

 **APPLE AMBROSIA** *Makes 4-6 servings*

Sweetened condensed milk and lime make this ambrosia different. Mixing sweet and tart apple varieties will also give it zing!

> 1 can (14 oz.) sweetened condensed milk
> 1 cup plain yogurt
> ½ cup lime juice
> 1 tbs. grated fresh lime peel (zest)
> 1½ cups chopped apples with peel
> 1 can (21 oz.) pineapple chunks, drained
> 1 can (11 oz.) mandarin oranges, drained
> ½ cup flaked coconut
> ½ cup white miniature marshmallows
> ½ cup chopped pecans, toasted

In a bowl, combine milk, yogurt, lime juice and lime rind and mix well. Add remaining ingredients and stir to combine. Chill for several hours before serving.

APPLET CANDY

This popular, wholesome soft candy is easy to make.

4 apples, peeled, cored and thinly
  sliced
water to cover
2 tbs. Knox gelatin

2 cups sugar
1 cup chopped walnuts, toasted
2 tsp. vanilla extract
confectioners' sugar for rolling

Place apples and water in a saucepan, bring to a boil, reduce heat and simmer until apples are very tender, about 15 minutes. Puree in a blender or food processor until smooth. You will need about 1¼ cups applesauce to make candies. Mix ½ cup cold applesauce with gelatin and allow to stand for 15 minutes.

In a saucepan, combine ¾ cup applesauce and sugar and bring to a boil, add gelatin mixture and cook for 15 minutes. Remove from heat, stir in walnuts and vanilla, and pour into a buttered 8-inch square pan. Refrigerate for several hours, cut into squares and roll in powdered sugar.

APPLESAUCE

*By using different varieties of apples and playing with the spices,
you can create endless applesauce taste sensations!*

1 lb. apples, peeled, cored and sliced
2 tbs. lemon juice
3 tbs. butter
½-1 cup white or brown sugar, or to taste
pinch cinnamon
pinch nutmeg and/or pinch cloves, optional

Place apples, lemon juice, butter, sugar and spices of choice in a saucepan and cook over low heat until apples are soft. Gently cut into small pieces for a chunky applesauce or place in a food processor or blender and blend until smooth. Taste and adjust seasonings.

RUM-GLAZED APPLES

*This can be used as a topping for breakfast pancakes, as a side dish
for spicy meat dishes or as a dessert, served over ice cream.*

4 cups sliced peeled tart apples
1 tbs. lemon juice
3 tbs. butter, melted
1 cup white sugar or firmly packed brown sugar
3 tbs. dark rum

Mix apples with lemon juice and place in shallow baking dish. Drizzle
with melted butter and bake in a 350° oven for 20 minutes. Remove pan
from oven and sprinkle apples with sugar and rum. Place under a broiler
until glazed (watch very carefully). Serve immediately.

# APPLE BUTTER

Makes 6 cups

Spicy apple jam is reminiscent of a dark applesauce. Newton Pippin apples are best, but you are not limited to this variety.

5 lb. apples, peeled and cored
7½ cups water
2 cups apple cider vinegar
1-2 cups brown sugar, or to taste

1½ tsp. cinnamon
1 tsp. ground cloves
1 tsp. allspice
½ tsp. nutmeg

Cut apples into thin slices and place in heavy saucepan with water and ¼ cup of the vinegar. Bring to a boil and cook for 20 minutes. Remove from heat and puree apples and water in a food processor or blender. Place remaining vinegar in a saucepan, boil and reduce to 1 cup. Add vinegar and remaining ingredients to pureed apples. Simmer gently for 30 minutes or until thickened.

Pour mixture into a glass baking dish. Bake in a 250° oven for 6 hours, stirring occasionally. Spoon into sterilized jars and heat seal or keep in the refrigerator until ready to use.

APPLE PEAR SAUCE

*This sauce is good served as an accompaniment to pork,
chicken and beef dishes.*

3 tart apples, peeled, cored and chopped
3 ripe pears, peeled, cored and chopped
1 cup dry white wine
¼ cup Calvados, apple brandy or cognac
½ cup brown sugar, firmly packed
1 tsp. dry mustard
¼ tsp. cinnamon
pinch nutmeg
pinch ground cloves

Place all ingredients in a heavy nonaluminum saucepan, bring to a
boil, reduce heat and simmer until fruit is tender, about 25 minutes.
Pour mixture into a food processor or blender and puree until smooth.
Taste and adjust sweetness and seasonings.

INDEX